WORLD EXPLORERS

Travels to Distant Lands

1000–1400

Stephen Currie

PICTURE CREDITS

Cover (back), 14 (top left), 16 (left), 30 (top right), 32 DK Images; cover Scala/Art Resource, NY; cover (top right), 3 (top left), 6 (bottom left), 9 (bottom right), 11 (bottom right), 31 (bottom right) Werner Forman/Art Resource, NY; 1, 4–5 (bottom) The Bodleian Library, University of Oxford (Ms.Ashmole 1511, fol. 86v); 2 Asian Art & Archaeology, Inc./Corbis; 3 Mary Evans Picture Library; 4 (top left), 8 (top left), 30 (top left) Reuters NewMedia Inc./Corbis; 4–5 (top) Yann Arthus Bertrand/Corbis; 4 (bottom), 20 Bibliotheque Nationale, Paris/Archives Charmet/Bridgeman Art Library; 5 (bottom left), 28–29 (bottom) Photodisc; 5 (bottom middle) Galen Rowell/Corbis; 5 (bottom right) Corbis; 6 (left) The Pierpont Morgan Library/Art Resource, NY; 6–7 Wayne Mcloughlin/National Geographic Image Collection; 9 (bottom) Hulton Archive/Getty Images; 10 Nasjonalgalleriet, Oslo, Norway/Bridgeman Art Library; 11 (top) Tom Lovell/National Geographic Image Collection; 12 Louis S. Glanzman/National Geographic Image Collection; 13 (left) Tim Thompson/Corbis; 13 (right) National Museum of Denmark; 14 (bottom) The Bodleian Library, University of Oxford (Ms.BODL.264, fol.218r); 15, 17 Michael Yamashita; 16 (right) Victoria and Albert Museum, London/Art Resource, NY; 18 Art Resource, NY; 19 (left) Giraudon/ Art Resource, NY; 19 (right) Private Collection/Bridgeman Art Library; 21 (left) Raymond Gehman/Corbis; 21 (right) Dallas and John Heaton/Corbis; 22 (top left), 27, 29 James L. Stanfield/National Geographic Image Collection; 22 (bottom) W. Robert Moore/National Geographic/Getty Images; 23 AFP/Corbis; 24 Arne Hodalic/Corbis; 25, 26 Burt Silverman/National Geographic Image Collection; 28–29 David G. Houser/Corbis; 30 (right) Peter Christopher

Produced through the worldwide resources of the National Geographic Society, John M. Fahey, Jr., President and Chief Executive Officer; Gilbert M. Grosvenor, Chairman of the Board; Nina D. Hoffman, Executive Vice President and President, Books and Education Publishing Group.

PREPARED BY NATIONAL GEOGRAPHIC SCHOOL PUBLISHING
Ericka Markman, Senior Vice President and President, Children's Books and Education Publishing Group; Steve Mico, Vice President, Editorial Director; Marianne Hiland, Executive Editor; Anita Schwartz, Project Editor; Jim Hiscott, Design Manager; Kristin Hanneman, Illustrations Manager; Diana Bourdrez, Picture Editor; Matt Wascavage, Manager of Publishing Services; Sean Philpotts, Production Manager.

MANUFACTURING AND QUALITY MANAGEMENT
Christopher A. Liedel, Chief Financial Officer; Phillip L. Schlosser, Director; Clifton M. Brown, Manager.

ART DIRECTION
Dan Banks, Project Design Company

CONSULTANT/REVIEWER
Dr. Margit E. McGuire, School of Education, Seattle University, Seattle, Washington

BOOK DEVELOPMENT
Nieman Inc.

BOOK DESIGN
Three Communication Design, LLC

PICTURE EDITING AND MANAGEMENT
Corrine L. Brock/In the Lupe, Inc.

MAP DEVELOPMENT AND PRODUCTION
Elizabeth Wolf

Published by the National Geographic Society
1145 17th Street, N.W.
Washington, D.C. 20036-4688

ISBN: 0-7922-4542-3

Printed in Canada

cover: caravan in the desert; (top right) Viking coins
page 1: Viking ship on top of a huge fish
page 2: Chinese vase from the time of Kublai Khan
page 3 (top): Viking brooch; (bottom): Kublai Khan hunting

Table of Contents

Introduction
The World in 1000 4

Chapter 1
The Viking Who Sailed
to America 8

Chapter 2
The Merchant Who Traveled
to China 14

Chapter 3
The Pilgrim Who Wandered
the World 22

Changes
The World in 1400 30

Glossary 31

Index 32

The World
in 1000

Most people who lived in the year 1000 knew very little about the lands beyond the nearby woods and fields. They made up stories about what other countries might be like. They told of boiling seas, of strange people with only one leg or the heads of dogs.

They told of dragons and giants, and sea monsters as big as ships. It was a big and frightening world out there! Even learned men didn't know much more. Their maps showed the outlines of some lands fairly well. The best maps were still full of guesses.

How far south did Africa go? What lay west of Spain? No one knew for sure. One reason for all this guesswork was that in 1000 and for centuries afterward very few people traveled. One person who did was Leif Ericsson, a **Viking** who sailed from Greenland to North America around 1000. About 270 years later, Marco Polo journeyed from Italy to China. And in 1325, a young man named Ibn Battuta began 30 years of wandering through Asia and Africa.

Few people traveled because getting around was very hard. Travelers of the time could go by land or by sea. Neither was easy, pleasant, or even safe. Most roads were terrible—dusty in summer and muddy in winter. When people had to travel long distances across harsh country, such as a desert, they could join a camel caravan. Camels can carry heavy loads and endure great heat and cold.

◀ Europeans thought that dog-headed people lived in the East.

Voyage of
Leif Ericsson

Marco Polo's
return to
Venice

Ibn Battuta's return
to Morocco

First voyage
of Christopher
Columbus

| 1000 | 1100 | 1200 | 1300 | 1400 | 1500 |

Going by sea was usually faster than going by land, but not always. The winds might be blowing the wrong way, or not all. Sailing across open water without a compass was risky, so people stayed close to shore. Besides, boats were small and cramped, and they could spring leaks.

Vikings raiding a coastal town by ship

In 1000, Viking ships were the best in the world. The Vikings, or Norsemen, were seafaring people from northern Europe. Between about 800 and 1100, they **raided**, traded, and settled over a wide area, from Greenland to Russia. The most famous type of Viking ship was the **longship**. Long, narrow, and very fast, these ships were built for raiding.

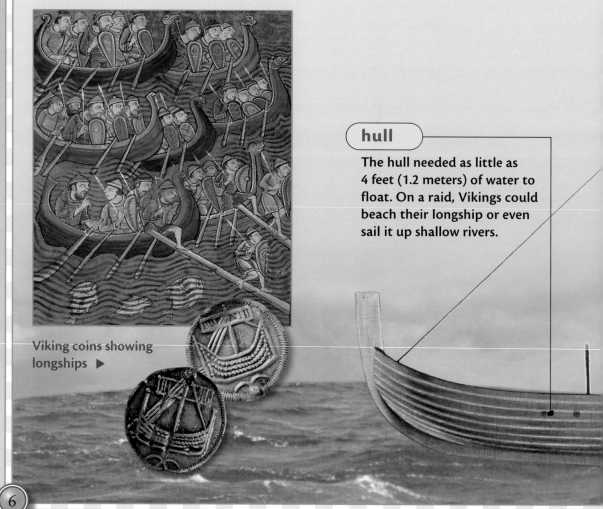

hull

The hull needed as little as 4 feet (1.2 meters) of water to float. On a raid, Vikings could beach their longship or even sail it up shallow rivers.

Viking coins showing longships ▶

A Viking Longship

Viking longship, 75 feet (23 meters)

school bus, 36 feet (11 meters)

sail

Viking women wove sails from wool or linen. With a steady breeze, a longship could reach a speed of almost 14 miles (23 kilometers) per hour.

mast

The mast was taken down in rough weather so it would not break. To replace a mast during a raid would be a problem.

rudder

The rudder made a longship easy to maneuver.

Chapter 1

The Viking Who Sailed to America

*A*round the year 1000, a small boat sliced through the icy waters of the North Atlantic Ocean. The captain of the boat was a brave Viking named Leif Ericsson. Leif was heading west across the ocean and into the unknown. His voyage would take him to North America.

What was a Viking? In Leif's time, the word "Viking" was sure to fill most Europeans with dread. Viking raiders attacked towns from the sea, stealing whatever they could and killing those who fought back. The French even added a new prayer to their church services: "From the fury of the Vikings, save us, O Lord!" But some Vikings, like Leif, also settled new lands.

Leif was born in Iceland, an island far out in the North Atlantic. The Vikings had settled Iceland around 850. Leif grew up learning about boats and the sea. He soon became a fine sailor with a zest for adventure. Even before he sailed to North America, Leif had made dangerous trips to Norway and to Greenland, a huge island further to the west. Leif's father, Erik the Red, had been the first Viking to settle in Greenland.

Erik had been forced to leave Iceland after killing several of his neighbors during quarrels. Before long, about 3,000 Vikings had moved to Greenland. Leif also joined his father there.

Leif Ericsson's World
➡ Leif's Voyage to Vinland, 1000

GREENLAND

ICELAND

...Island)
...LLULAND)

NORWAY

SWEDEN

Erik's Settlement

NORTH

ATLANTIC

OCEAN

SCOTLAND

North Sea

RTH

Labrador
(MARKLAND)

ERICA

L'Anse aux Meadows

IRELAND

ENGLAND

Newfoundland
(VINLAND)

FRANCE

Kilometers
0   500   1000

Miles
0   500   1000

N
W   E
S

Vikings in battle with the English

Viking helmet

Leif Sails West

A few years after the Greenland settlement was started, a Viking got blown off course while sailing there. When he finally arrived, he said he had seen strange new lands farther to the west. His tale made Leif curious. In about 1000, Leif decided to sail west to see what he could find. The Viking **sagas,** or stories of their ancient heroes, say that about 20 or 30 men joined Leif.

They sailed west across the unknown ocean, using sails when they could and rowing when they couldn't. After days of travel, they came upon a flat and icy coastline, which Leif called Helluland, "Flat Stone Land." There was not much there, and no good reason to stay, so Leif and his men headed farther south. Before long, they ran into land again, but this coast was different.

Leif pointing to the coast of North America

Vikings landing in Vinland

This land had wide, sandy beaches and many trees, so Leif named it Markland, "Woodland." The Vikings sailed back into the open ocean, and turned south once more. When they landed again, for the third and last time, they were at a place that Leif liked even better than Markland.

This land was hilly and also covered with trees. There were very few trees in Iceland or Greenland. So the Vikings eagerly cut down some of the biggest trees to bring home for lumber. The men also noticed that wheat, fruit, and other plants grew very well. Leif called the place Vinland, "Vineland." They stayed for the winter, but in the spring they headed home again.

Where was Vinland? Over the years, many people have tried to locate it. In 1961, scientists found the ruins of a Viking settlement at a site called L'Anse aux Meadows in Newfoundland, Canada. Was that Vinland? Today, most people believe it probably was. So far, no one can be sure.

Viking ship anchor

Vikings in Vinland

Leif Ericsson and his men were not the last Vikings to see Vinland. His brother Thorvald led another voyage there a year or so later. Thorvald stayed for two years, but then he was killed in a fight with some Native Americans. The rest of his men escaped and returned to Greenland.

Later still, another group of Vikings went to Vinland. They were led by a Viking named Thorfinn. He had married Gudrid, the widow of one of Erik's sons. Gudrid and a few other women went on this voyage. They planned to settle in Vinland, just as earlier Vikings had settled in Iceland and Greenland.

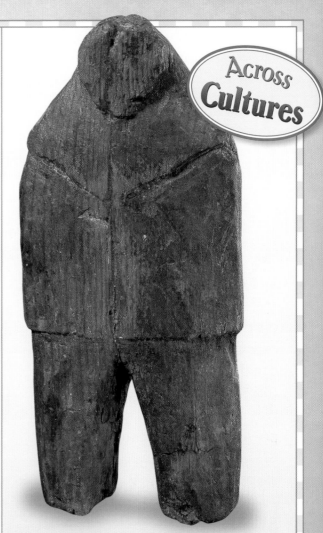

Across Cultures

Thorfinn and Gudrid had a baby boy during their first year in Vinland. They named the child Snorri. The Viking settlement did not last. No one knows just why. Maybe Vinland was too far from Greenland and Iceland. Maybe the Vikings were driven out by Native Americans. Whatever the reason, the settlers vanished not long after they came.

Interior of a restored Viking house at L'Anse aux Meadows

Inuit people were living on Greenland when the Vikings were there. These early Native Americans left no written records about their contacts with the Vikings. The Inuit did leave carvings like this one. Some people today think that these carvings show how the Inuit saw the Vikings.

Chapter 2

The Merchant Who Traveled to China

Venice is a beautiful city in northern Italy. Some of the major "roads" in Venice are actually **canals**, or waterways built for travel. In the late 1200s, Venice was one of the world's most powerful cities because of trade.

Some trade goods came from as far away as India and China. They were passed from one trader to another, and finally brought to Europe. Many of the goods came through Venice. Trade had made the city very rich.

The Polos stand next to Venice's Grand Canal as they get ready to leave for China.

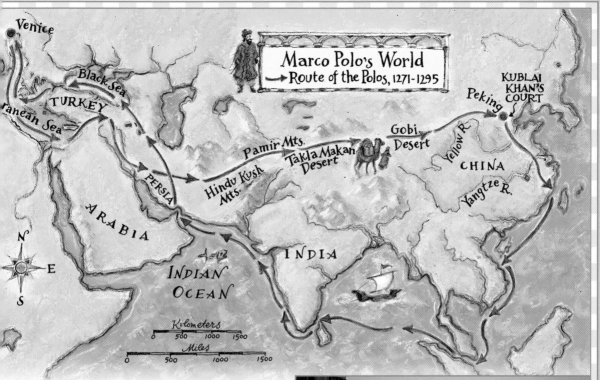

Marco Polo's World
→ Route of the Polos, 1271-1295

Venice

Black Sea

TURKEY

...ranean Sea

PERSIA

ARABIA

Hindu Kush Mts.

Pamir Mts.

Takla Makan Desert

Gobi Desert

Yellow R.

Peking

KUBLAI KHAN'S COURT

CHINA

Yangtze R.

INDIA

INDIAN OCEAN

Kilometers
0   500   1000   1500

Miles
0   500   1000   1500

N E S W

Most people in Venice didn't know where all these goods came from. At least one man was eager to find out. He was a **merchant** named Niccolo Polo. With his brother, Maffeo, he took a trip to Turkey in about 1254. From there, the Polo brothers headed east.

The Polos hoped to make it as far as China—and they did. They stayed in Asia for about 15 years. After they returned home, Niccolo and Maffeo did not stay long in Venice. They soon decided to make another trip to the East. This time they brought along Niccolo's 17-year-old son, Marco.

Then & NOW

Venice's Grand Canal still looks a lot like the spot from which the Polos set out on their journey to China. But today, motorboats cruise alongside Venice's famous single-oared boats called gondolas.

Along the Silk Road

Niccolo, Maffeo, and Marco traveled east across Asia along the **Silk Road**. The Silk Road was a network of trade routes that went from China all the way to Europe. The merchants who traveled the route often carried silk, a cloth made in China. But traders brought other goods along the Silk Road too.

The Polos could travel safely because the **Mongols** kept peace along the Silk Road. The Mongols were a Central Asian people who conquered a huge empire in the early 1200s.

By the late 1200s, the Mongols controlled most of Asia—and almost all of the Silk Road. Although the Mongols were great **warriors**, or brave fighters, they saw the value of peace and trade. They stopped the fighting along the Silk Road and patrolled the route to make sure that merchants were safe from robbers. Under Mongol rule, people said, a girl with a bag of gold in her hand could walk in safety from one end of the Silk Road to the other.

Chinese silk

Mongol horseman

Pamir Mountains

As he traveled, Marco saw strange sights. In one place, oil seeped out of the ground. In another, the Polos crossed a desert of salt. Later, they climbed the very high Pamir Mountains.

Marco noticed that fire did not burn as brightly or cook food as well. He thought it was the cold (rather than lack of oxygen) that caused this to happen. The Polos did not reach China for three and a half years.

The Wonders of China

The emperor of China was a Mongol named Kublai Khan (KOO-bli KAHN). When the Polos arrived in China, they went to visit the emperor at his royal court. Kublai Khan was very pleased to see these travelers. He wanted to know all about life in Europe, and he asked them many questions about their journey.

Kublai Khan was interested in Niccolo and Maffeo, but he was especially impressed with Marco. He found the young man smart and thoughtful. In turn, Marco thought that the Mongol emperor was brave and wise. The two men soon became friends, although Marco was barely 20 years old and Kublai Khan was about 60.

Kublai Khan giving the Polos his golden seal to allow them to travel in his empire

When the emperor asked Marco to join his court, Marco quickly agreed. It is not clear today exactly how Marco Polo served Kublai Khan. We know he traveled a lot.

Perhaps Marco delivered messages for the emperor. Or perhaps he took Kublai Khan's place when he could not go to important meetings himself. In any case, Marco visited many other places while a member of the court. His duties took him throughout Kublai Khan's vast empire. Wherever he went, he watched—and learned.

Chinese paper money

Marco Polo was amazed that the Chinese used paper money, which was unknown in Europe. The Chinese, he wrote, made "the bark of a certain tree into something resembling sheets of paper, but black." The paper was then inked to show its value and to prove that it was real. People used this paper money all through the Mongol Empire as if it were gold. Marco thought paper money was a wonderful idea. After all, he wrote, "it is vastly lighter to carry about."

Marco Polo dressed as a Mongol

Coming Home

By about 1286, the Polos were ready to leave China. They were homesick for Venice. Kublai Khan acted hurt when they asked him if they could go. For several years, he refused to give them permission. Because the emperor was so powerful, the Polos knew they had to obey.

Why were they finally able to leave? In 1291, a Chinese princess needed to travel to Persia, now called Iran, to marry a prince. Kublai wanted to make sure she got there safely, so he asked the Polos to bring her to her new husband. After that, he agreed, they could go home if they liked.

The Polos brought home gems like these.

◄ The Polos returned home by sea.

This time, Marco, Niccolo, and Maffeo made the trip by sea. The voyage home took another three years. It is said that no one recognized the Polos when they got back to Venice at last! And no one believed their story until they did something wonderful. They ripped open the seams of their clothes and out fell hundreds of gems that they had sewed into the linings!

Soon after returning home, Marco joined Venice's navy and was taken prisoner after a sea battle. While in jail, he met a writer who thought that his story would make a great book. Marco agreed to try. Together, the two men wrote the story of his travels.

? It's a Mystery

One of the puzzles of Marco Polo's book is not what he put in, but what he left out. Among other things, Marco failed to mention the Chinese custom of binding women's feet to make them small. He never talked about how the Chinese used woodblocks for printing, or ate with chopsticks, or drank tea. Marco even left out the biggest thing in China—the Great Wall.

China's Great Wall

Chapter 3

The Pilgrim Who Wandered the World

Even in the days when hardly anyone traveled, some people—called **pilgrims**—still visited certain places for religious reasons. Lots of Christians, for instance, went to Rome. People of different faiths journeyed to Jerusalem. In the 1300s, the spot that drew the most pilgrims was probably the city of Mecca in Arabia.

Muslims are believers in Islam, the religion founded by Muhammad (moo-HAM-id). To Muslims, Mecca is a holy city. Indeed, all Muslims are supposed to go to Mecca sometime in their lives. This trip is called the *hajj*. Each year, Muslim pilgrims from many lands find a way to make the hajj.

Pilgrims had to cross a desert to reach Mecca.

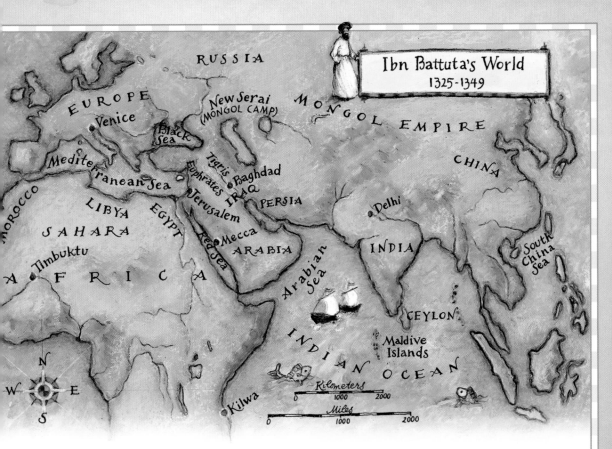

Ibn Battuta's World
1325-1349

In 1325, a young Muslim student named Ibn Battuta decided to go to Mecca. Ibn Battuta lived in the North African country of Morocco. The holy city was thousands of miles away, but Ibn Battuta was eager to go. One day, he left his family and friends and journeyed east.

It took him a year and a half to get to Mecca. When he was done with his pilgrimage, he decided not to go home, but to travel the entire Muslim world. It would be nearly 25 years before he saw home again.

Walls surround Mecca's holiest shrine, the Kaaba.

A Wider World

In the next few years, Ibn Battuta traveled through much of the Middle East. He visited more holy places in Iraq and Persia. He saw the Euphrates River, which reminded him of a necklace. Then he went on to the Tigris River and saw the once-great city of Baghdad. It had been partly destroyed by the Mongols years before. By this time, Ibn Battuta had met hundreds of people. He hadn't exactly made friends with all of them. He preferred people who were well-educated and had good manners.

Ibn Battuta listened to almost everybody. Many people had told him about fascinating places elsewhere in the world. He was eager to see these places for himself.

So when Ibn Battuta was done exploring the Middle East, he still did not head for home. Instead, he took a ship south along the eastern coast of Africa. Ibn Battuta had never been on a ship so large, or one that traveled so far from land. He was terrified, but soon got used to sea travel.

Ibn Battuta sailed south along the African coast in this type of Arab sailing ship, called a dhow.

Ibn Battuta (center) visits the Mongol camp. A yurt pulled by horses is behind him.

He sailed as far south as Kilwa, a small island off the coast of what is now Tanzania. Ibn Battuta, who liked comfort, was delighted that the people of Kilwa had running water and three-story houses.

After visiting Africa, Ibn Battuta traveled far to the north. He visited the camp of a Mongol ruler of Russia. Like the people of Kilwa, the Mongols had interesting houses.

The Mongols lived in **yurts**, which are tents made of felt mounted on large wagons. They could move them whenever they wanted.

One thing Ibn Battuta didn't like about Russia was the winter cold. "I used to put on three fur coats and two pairs of trousers," he wrote. The outfit kept him warm, but made him so bulky he had to be lifted onto his horse!

India and Beyond

One night, Ibn Battuta was the guest of a holy man. Ibn Battuta dreamed that a giant bird carried him to India, far to the east. When he awoke, he was amazed to find that the holy man already knew what he had dreamed. Both men were sure that someday Ibn Battuta would visit this mysterious land.

Ibn Battuta did exactly that—although he traveled on horseback, not birdback. He liked India so much that he gave up wandering for a while. During the next eight years, he served as a judge at the court of India's **sultan,** or ruler.

Ibn Battuta kissing the hand of the Indian sultan

Adam's Peak on the island of Ceylon

Ibn Battuta wrote that the Indian sultan was a strange man—both kind and cruel. "There was no day that the gate of his palace did not see his gift of riches to one person and his torture and murder of another."

In 1341, the sultan sent Ibn Battuta to China to represent him. Ibn Battuta started off in style. He had with him 1,000 horsemen and two enormous ships. But the ships sank before he got very far, drowning almost all his men. Instead of telling the sultan, he left for China on his own.

Ibn Battuta got there—but first, of course, he wandered. He visited the Maldive Islands in the Indian Ocean, Ceylon (now Sri Lanka), and parts of Southeast Asia.

Even though he had worked hard to get there, Ibn Battuta didn't think much of China. Perhaps the problem was that China had almost no Muslims. Ibn Battuta traveled mainly in Muslim lands, and he had a hard time understanding the ways and customs of other people. "China was beautiful," he wrote, "but it did not please me."

The Wanderer Returns

Ibn Battuta left China in 1346. Finally, he was heading back home to Morocco. It was his own land, he wrote, and that made it "better than any other country." But being Ibn Battuta, he stopped often along the way. The journey took more than three years.

Once he was home, Ibn Battuta was still not done traveling. A few years later, he made one last great journey south into Africa. He went 1,500 miles (2,400 kilometers) to the African kingdom of Mali, south of the great desert of the Sahara. Mali was one of the few Muslim countries that he had not yet visited.

Ibn Battuta traveled across the Sahara on camels.

Ibn Battuta liked some of what he saw. He thought that Mali's emperor was a good ruler—but stingy. Ibn Battuta hoped the emperor would welcome him with rich gifts of fine robes and gold. Instead, he got bread and yogurt. Ibn Battuta soon returned home. This time he decided to stay.

The king of Morocco took an interest in Ibn Battuta's travels. He ordered Ibn Battuta to write up his adventures with the help of a secretary. The book took almost two years to write. Like Marco Polo's book, it has some parts that sound made up. But like Marco Polo's book, it is mostly true.

This Muslim house of worship in Mali was built around the time Ibn Battuta was there.

The World in 1400

ow did Leif Ericsson, Marco Polo, and Ibn Battuta change the way people saw the world? Leif's discovery of America had little effect. The sagas that recorded the Vikings' trips to North America were read only by other Vikings. The influence of Ibn Battuta was far greater. The book of his travels was well known throughout the Muslim world.

Marco Polo's journeys had a very big effect. They helped Christopher Columbus decide to sail west across the Atlantic. Columbus's copy of Marco's book still exists. It's full of Columbus's careful notes. He was very interested, for example, in what Marco said about the palace of the Japanese king. Marco said that his palace had floors of gold "two fingers thick."

Marco Polo's journeys inspired Columbus to sail across the Atlantic.

All these travelers showed an eagerness to learn about what lay beyond the horizon. In the years after 1400, many explorers would follow their lead. In time, people would come to know much more about the rest of the world.

Glossary

canal a waterway built for travel

longship a long, narrow, swift warship used by Viking raiders

merchant a person who buys and sells goods for a living

Mongols a Central Asian people who conquered a huge empire in the early 1200s

Muslims believers in Islam, the religion founded by Muhammad

pilgrim a person who travels for religious reasons

raid to make a surprise attack

saga a Viking story of ancient heroes

Silk Road a network of trade routes that went from China all the way to Europe

sultan a ruler in India

Vikings seafaring people from Northern Europe who raided, traded, and settled over a wide area between about 800 and 1100

warrior brave fighter

yurt a tent mounted on a wagon and used as a house by the Mongols

This carved dragon head comes from a Viking ship.

Index

Africa 5, 23–25

China 5, 14–21, 27, 28

Columbus, Christopher 5, 30

Ericsson, Leif 5, 8–12, 30

Erik the Red 8–9, 12

Greenland 5–6, 8–13

Helluland 9–10

Ibn Battuta 5, 22–30

Iceland 8–9, 11–13

India 14–15, 23, 26

Kilwa 23, 25

Kublai Khan 18–20

L'Anse aux Meadows 9, 11, 13

longships 6–7, 31

Maldive Islands 23, 27

Mali 23, 28–29

Markland 9, 11

Mecca 22–23

Mongols 16, 18–19, 25, 31

Morocco 23, 28–29

Muhammad 22

Muslims 22–23, 27, 28, 31

Native Americans 12–13

North America 8–10

Polo, Maffeo 15–18, 20–21

Polo, Marco 5, 15–21, 29–30

Polo, Niccolo 15–18, 20–21

Russia 6, 23, 25

sagas 10, 30–31

Silk Road 16, 31

Snorri 13

Turkey 15

Venice 14–15, 20–21

Vikings 6–13, 30–31

Vinland 9, 11–13

yurts 25, 31